C000196111

CHICHESTER HARBOUR

PAST & PRESENT

*A collection of photographs old and new,
of the Harbour villages of Nutbourne, Chidham,
Bosham, Fishbourne, Appledram, Dell Quay,
Birdham, Itchenor & West Wittering.*

by

Angela Bromley-Martin

HUGHENDEN PUBLICATIONS

Bibliography

Victoria County History of Sussex
Bosham Church: Its History and Antiquities by K.H. MacDermott
Fishbourne: A Village History by Rita Blakeney
South Eastern Sail by Michael Bouquet
A History of Sussex by J.R. Armstrong

Published by
HUGHENDEN PUBLICATIONS

ISBN 0-9517533-1-2

© 1991 Angela Bromley-Martin

All rights reserved. No part of this publication may be reproduced, stored in a retrieval system, or transmitted in any form or by any means, electronic, mechanical, photocopying, recording or otherwise, without the prior permission of the copyright owner.

Designed by
DIANA GREENWOOD MEAD

Typeset by
ARTICULATE STUDIO

Printed by
BILLINGS & SON, WORCESTER

CONTENTS

INTRODUCTION

THE inspiration for this book was prompted by my introduction to John and Ruth Wakeford who had found, in John's grandfather's house, a box of some 400 glass negatives taken, it would appear, between the years 1901-1911. It seemed a pity that these old photographs should not reach a wider public and so was conceived the idea of producing a book, using some of these old photographs and, where it was possible, showing beside each old photograph the same view as it is today, some 90 years later.

The photographs were principally of the area between Nutbourne and Fishbourne and included Bosham and Chidham, an area which would not have in itself been sufficient for a book. So it was decided to make the book of all the Chichester Harbour villages in West Sussex.

The gentleman (for we assume him to be male, as there were few female photographers around at that time) was thought to have been John Bell Metcalfe who lived in Hampstead House, an 18th-century farmhouse on the main road in Chidham, now a steak house called The Bosham Inn. A great majority of the photographs was taken at "Oaklands", two doors away from Hampstead House, and which was purchased by the Misses Metcalfe in 1901. The Misses Metcalfe are thought to have been the sisters and an aunt of John Bell Metcalfe.

The glass negatives were found in Prospect Farm, a few doors away from Oaklands, which had belonged to Amos Wakeford, grandfather of John Wakeford.

James II (1633-1701) granted the City of Chichester a Charter for Chichester Harbour which gave the City the right to collect all the harbour dues. The designated area for Chichester Harbour was then given as from Hermitage on the Sussex/Hampshire border near Emsworth as the north-westerly point, as far south of the harbour mouth between West Wittering and Hayling Island as a horn blown at the harbour mouth could be heard. From thence the border went eastwards to Selsey, Pagham and the Parish of Felpham and finally northwards to Dell Quay, the port for Chichester. This book will not include those villages that are not adjacent to the harbour.

I am greatly indebted and would like to thank the Wakefords for all their help. In addition I should also like to thank the following:

Mr Martin Hayes, Principal Librarian of Local Studies of the West Sussex Library
Mr & Mrs K. Haines
Mr & Mrs G. Haines
Mr & Mrs K. Smith
Miss Olive Willshire and Mrs Ethel Lambeth (née Willshire)
Mr T. Baxendale
Mr S. Roth

Finally I am grateful for the help given to me by Mr Geoffrey Marwood and the late Mr Martin Beale in going through the proofs for me and correcting any mistakes I made, both historically and grammatically.

This is probably a family snap of the Metcalfe family, with the three Misses Metcalfe, the photographer himself – John Bell Metcalfe, back right – with another relative. Amongst the negatives there is a number of photographs of this gentleman, sometimes in clerical collar.

HISTORY

IT IS only quite recently in the history of the earth – a mere 10,000 years – that the inlets of Chichester Harbour were formed. The English Channel was previously a river into which flowed the Solent River of which the creeks of Chichester Harbour formed a part. Now Chichester Harbour is a tidal inlet.

The Arrival of the Romans

Through the centuries, thick oak forests grew up around the shores and these, together with the heavy clay soil, would have made habitation hard until man could make iron tools with which to cut down the oaks and dig the soil. Then full use could be made of the excellent soil for growing corn, the oaks could be used for house and boat building and the acorns were food for the swine.

Although the Belgae and the Celts had occupied this area, it is the Romans who were the first known people who really left their mark on Chichester Harbour. In A.D. 43 the Romans arrived, under the direction of Vespasian and settled at the top of what is now known as Fishbourne Creek, north of Dell Quay. The vast buildings found at Fishbourne, which started off as barracks to house men and equipment for the Roman conquest of the west country of England and were to become the Palace of King Cogidubnus, are evidence of the importance of Chichester Harbour to the Romans.

The Romans departed from England in the 5th Century, leaving the country to the Saxons as well as Angles and Jutes. The Saxons were principally farmers and, probably for defensive reasons, were disinclined to occupy the towns left by the Romans but settled into little farming communities in areas where there were the necessities for their form of life – woods, good soil and water. For those settling around Chichester Harbour there would have been the added advantage of fishing. It is interesting to note that in the 8th Century, Bosham was the sixth most important town in Sussex, while Dell Quay was the seventh.

The Vikings

The Vikings, who were given to raiding all along the coast, are said to have come into Chichester Harbour many times; in fact it is chronicled that they attacked Chichester in 840 A.D. and 895 A.D. but were repulsed on both occasions.

Alfred the Great (849-899 A.D.) was so infuriated by these continual raids by the Vikings that he had built a number of fortified towns or burhs, one of which was at Chichester.

The Danish King Canute is reputed to have had a manor house at Bosham which would have been only a day's ride from his capital at Winchester. The manor passed to Godwin, who was the father of Harold and father-in-law of Edward the Confessor. Recent research shows that Edward the Confessor was a good king, even if he did lead a somewhat monastic existence. He would appear to have given his father-in-law tremendous powers and was also greatly influenced by him. Godwin did, however, quarrel with his son-in-law in 1052 and was forced to flee the country, sailing from Thorney Island with his wife and two of their sons. The quarrel must

Part of the Bayeux Tapestry showing Harold setting forth from Bosham in 1064

have been short-lived for Godwin returned the following year.

Shown in the Bayeux Tapestry, an 11th-century embroidery of the history of the Norman invasion of England, is King Harold setting forth from Bosham in 1064 to visit William of Normandy. After the battle of Hastings, where Harold was killed and William took over the crown of England, William used Chichester Harbour as his main port and base for communication with Normandy. Chichester Harbour is in a strategic position in relation to the coast of Normandy, for the prevailing winds of the English Channel are south-westerly, so with the type of boat and sails that were available then, travelling between Normandy and Chichester Harbour would have been comparatively simple so long as the wind remained in the south-west.

Domesday

King William was soon busy re-organising his new kingdom; he ordered the compilation of the Domesday Book, which was a register for taxation purposes of all land and property in the kingdom. Bosham is shown as one of the wealthiest manors in England and included Appledram, Chidham and Thorney.

Although it is known that at least one ship went from Chichester Harbour to fight the Spanish during the Spanish Armada, from then on Chichester Harbour does not appear significantly in history until the two great wars. There was an airfield at Chidham during the First World War. In the 1939-45 war, there was the R.A.F. Bomber Command Station at Thorney Island with decoys of wooden Spitfires sighted on East Head and decoy lights at Cobnor. There was also a small airfield at Appledram. (This is now the site of the Museum of D-Day Aviation.) Chichester Harbour also played a vital part in the D-Day landings in Normandy, when the entire harbour was filled with every imaginable type of craft necessary for the landings.

Administration of Chichester Harbour

Chichester Harbour had been administered, since the time of James II by the Chichester Corporation, but by the 1960s, it was plain that with the increasing number of pleasure yachts and a declining commercial trade a more constructive form of administration was needed to cover both the Sussex and Hampshire sectors of the harbour. Thus by Act of Parliament in 1971 the Chichester Harbour Conservancy was formed with the object of conserving, maintaining and improving the harbour and surrounding area while providing for "the occupation of leisure and recreation and the conservation of nature". This included not only that part of the harbour covered by this book, but included the Hampshire part of the harbour as far west as Langstone. Now the Manager/Harbour Master manages the area and is responsible to the Harbour Conservancy on which sit representatives from both Hampshire and West Sussex. The area has been designated an Area of Outstanding Natural Beauty and a Site of Special Scientific Interest (SSSI) as well as a Conservation Area.

'The Transit' built at Itchenor in 1800

VILLAGE LIFE

A corner of Bosham Lane, with the former Congregational Chapel, now the United Reformed Church, with Chapel Cottage, the U.F.C. Hall and Brooklyn Cottage looking much the same. The two barns shown on either side of the old photograph (one of them behind the blossom on the right) have now been demolished.

The little girl in the old picture is believed to be the daughter of Ernest Trevett who owned the house on the right (out of the picture) then called The Grange. This building is now the Millstream Hotel, although the waterway, which did provide the mill with its water power, has always been known as The Brook.

The waterfront of Bosham beside Quay Meadow. Little has changed; there were fewer but larger vessels at the turn of the century when Bosham was a commercial port. Today the large number of boats are now recreational yachts and Bosham has become a centre for dinghy sailing.

In the early 1920s the 'Prince of Wales' was launched in this creek of Bosham. Built for the Southend Navigation Co. to operate in the Thames, she was then the largest flat-bottomed passenger vessel in the world. To conform to Board of Trade regulations she had to be built under cover, so the buildings on the right of the old photo were built. These buildings were burnt down in the 1960s, although the area continued to be used as a yacht repair yard until 1989 when permission was given for the construction of four houses with garages.

ACROSS THE HARBOUR, OLD BOSHAM.

The waterfront of Bosham, which has changed little over the years. The only major change has been the demolition of the oyster barn to the right of the sailing boat in the old photo. A house called 'Oysters' now stands where the old building stood. The old barn, in addition to being used for the packing of oysters, was used once a week by the West Ashling butcher to sell meat. It was also where, before the Congregational Church was built in Bosham Lane in 1837, the non-conformists held their Sunday services.

THE SHORE, LOW TIDE, BOSHAM.

The waterfront of Bosham looking east, which from this angle has changed a great deal. All the houses on the left were occupied by fishermen who kept their boats anchored off their houses or, in bad weather, pulled them up the slips that were alongside the buildings. The rising high tide twice a day usually covers the road and at the very high spring tides twice a year, laps just below the lower windows. The modern photo shows the popularity of Bosham as a tourist attraction with the vast number of cars parked all along the shore. Some car owners, in spite of warning notices, fail to appreciate that at high tide, the time of which changes daily, their cars are liable to be submerged. In the summer it is a daily occurrence that a car is caught by the tide and frequently irreparably damaged as a result.

The Manor House of Bosham, the old photograph taken between 1920 and 1940. It is a moated house with water around 3½ sides of the present building. On the west side is the brook, some 10 or 12 feet above the level of the lawn.

Canute, Godwin and his son Harold are reputed to have had a manor here although the present building is largely 17th century, with a small section considerably older. There are, however, some Saxon walls and doorways in the garden, which suggest that there was a Saxon building of some sort south-west of the present house. The Manor House was at one time a farmhouse and an elderly lady born in 1881 told the author she remembered as a child seeing the farmer there dressed in a Sussex smock. The south wall of the Manor House garden is the north wall of the churchyard.

The High Street of Bosham, where one can just see, at the far end, the old sweet shop, still with its circular window in which were displayed the large bottles containing peppermints, toffees, etc. which were probably sold for about three or four sweets for an old halfpenny.

This building has now been divided into two houses. The one with the window, called Bay Tree House, is occupied by Mabel Stoveld, the daughter of the last shopkeeper here, Annie Stoveld.

On the left beyond the low wall are the two pubs, The Anchor and The Ship – the latter now a private house. Note the raised steps for entry into the cottages on the left; this is because at high spring tides, the sea water comes right up this street and would get into the houses and gardens but for these high steps and walls.

Hoe Farm House, Hoe Lane, Bosham. The Strange family arrived in Bosham in the early part of this century as farmers. Here are some of the family taken at Hoe Farm House in 1913, where Douglas Strange was born in 1916. Douglas Strange with his sons Richard and John still farm the area although the family no longer occupy this house. The mother of the photographer, Mrs Ferguson, is third from the left, while the Misses Strange stand by the front door.

Today the house is owned by Alex and Aileen Sandberg who, with one of their sons and his wife, pose outside a relatively unchanged building.

This building was bought by Lady Allen, who also at the time owned the whole of Bosham Hoe as well as Hoe Farm.

Many of the farm buildings, including a barn in front of the house, were almost flattened by the 1987 hurricane, which affected this part of Sussex so badly.

These three old photographs of The Swan at Bosham are from John Metcalfe's collection of negatives taken in the early 1900s.

The photo above left shows visitors arriving by carriage at The Swan on the old turnpike road that ran from Portsmouth to Chichester. The Swan was a coaching inn in the days when coaches ran from Portsmouth to Brighton and stopped here for a change of horses. The regular coach service stopped soon after the arrival of the trains in 1846.

The photo above right is in sharp contrast – a man pushes his handcart along the gravelled main road.

A different aspect of The Swan shows Station Road which runs alongside the pub. In the background can be seen the railway station. The board beside the man on the left is an advertisement for a railway excursion.

W. J. DURLING,

Wine and Spirit Merchant,

THE "SWAN HOTEL," BOSHAM.

Good Accommodation for Cyclists and Picnic Parties.

LUNCHEONS AND TEAS PROVIDED.

Good Stabling and Coach House Accommodation.

CHARGES REASONABLE.

BREAKFASTS
and SUPPERS
a Speciality

The Dutch Tea House

(Proprietress : Mrs. J. W. RUDDOCK)

BOSHAM

Telephone : BOSHAM 34

The old photo here shows a remover's wagon outside The Swan, with the village Pound on the left. The recent photograph shows the Indian Tandoori restaurant on the opposite corner to the pub. Some years ago this building was the Dutch Tea House. The road past the pub is now no longer the main coastal road so The Swan Inn has become a quiet country pub again and visitors can enjoy a meal outside, weather permitting, in comparative peace.

Church Lane, Bosham. Some years ago, Mrs Challis of the Mill House was given a short article, illustrated with photographs entitled 'Bosham–An Artists' Settlement'. Neither the author or the date are given, but one would guess that it was written in the late 1920s. One of the photos is of this artist sitting by the church gate with the path to the church on the right. On the left are 1 and 2 Church Cottages built in the last century on the site of the old College, occupied before the Reformation by Austin Canons. Today the two cottages have been converted into one house. The trees alas have fallen foul of either hurricane or disease and young trees are now growing in their place. Here, Mrs Beryl Biart takes her spaniel dog for his daily walk.

The Bayeux Tapestry, an historical embroidery commissioned by Queen Matilda, wife of William the Conqueror, shows the Chancel Arch of Bosham Church. Here Harold had a blessing service before setting out in his longboats for Normandy to parley with William over who should inherit the throne of England after the death of Edward the Confessor, Harold's brother-in-law.

In 1986, 25 ladies of the Bosham Women's Institute started an embroidered appliqué of 900 years of Bosham's history; this completed appliqué now hangs in Bosham Village Hall, which itself was built from funds raised by the same W.I. in 1924.

In the Domesday Book, a record of all land and property commissioned by William I, Bosham was one of the wealthiest manors in England at that time, and included some 11 mills, not all of them sited in Bosham. The Manor of Bosham then included property at Thorney, Itchenor and Appledram.

A corner of Bosham that has changed little over the years. The Congregational Church, built in 1837, is the same except for its name, now the United Reformed Church, with the church hall next door. The house on the right is still there, but not visible in the older photograph because of the trees. The gravel road has now been tarmacked and there are proper pavements.

The old Bosham village school was built in 1898, replacing the school that was built in 1834 at the top of School Rythe. The 1898 school became too small and in 1977 a new one was built on the same site. For a year, the school was accommodated in portacabins and the village hall. The one building that was not demolished was the Schoolmaster's house which can be seen on the right of both old and new photographs (top and bottom). The bell tower, which originated in the old school of 1834, was transferred to the 1898 school and can be seen on the left of the old photograph. It has now been placed on the newest school building and is on that section of the building that is out of the picture.

Broadstream Cottage, sometimes called Broadbridge Cottage, which is on the main road to the west of The Swan Inn, Bosham. Previously known as Pound Cottage, it is similar and believed to date from the same period as the cob-type Weaver's Cottage at the Weald and Downland Museum at Singleton, circa 1460. Over the years it has been in the possession of Frederick Fitzharding Maurice Berkeley, the Lord of the Manor of Bosham, as well as the Dean and Chapter of Chichester Cathedral, who let it to a John Pescett for £8.9.6d (about £8.50) per annum in 1880.

At the turn of the century it was occupied by a young lady with a small child. The young lady was said to be the mistress of a defrocked vicar who lived at Critchfield House in Bosham.

More recently, before the present owners purchased the house in 1970, it was known as the honeywoman's cottage. Here Mrs Clarke, who inherited the house from her husband, continued with the hives and sold the honey, as well as a few garden vegetables, from the window sill when the main road ran immediately outside the window. Today Dave and Irene Stunt (pictured in the modern photo) live in the cottage and have spent much time researching the history of their home.

Prospect Cottage, Chidham, which is printed from one of the negatives found in Prospect Farm next door. In this cottage Cecil and Kathleen Sopp (shown in the lower photograph) have lived since 1938. The main part of the cottage remains almost the same, but the Sopps have added on a single storied extension to the right.

'Oaklands', Chidham, was owned and occupied by the Misses Metcalfe at the time that the old photographs were taken – in fact it may well be that the ladies in the pictures are the Misses Metcalfe. It is thought that there were two Metcalfe sisters and their maiden aunt living in the house from 1901. The house was sold after the death of the last Miss Metcalfe in 1933. John Bell Metcalfe, who lived two doors away at Hampstead House, now Bosham Inn, was thought to be the brother of the two younger ladies and probably the photographer. (It is interesting to note that in the 1907 Electoral Roll, John Bell Metcalfe is given as the owner of Oaklands, while the Misses Metcalfe were given as the occupiers. Could it be that this was a way the ladies could have a vote, for it was not until 1918 that women had that right.)

Oaklands was one of four houses built by Mr Duffield in 1900. Colonel J.R. Matthews, who bought the house in 1970, removed much of the ornamentation of the house for ease of maintenance and painting. He has also replaced the Victorian sash windows with pvc double-glazed ones.

'Far Close', the house on the right, is next door to 'Oaklands' and was also built by Mr Duffield in 1900. The road it will be noticed in the old photograph is a gravel track, while today it is a main road with cars speeding past. There is not as much traffic as there was, for in 1988 a new by-pass was built, which left this road for local traffic; even so many cars use it daily.

The photo on the left is of Christmas Cottage which is alongside the Old Malt House – pictured below. Christmas Cottage has changed little over the years. Malt House Lane is now called Chidham Lane.

The main road at Chidham with the Old Malt House, which is now Chidham Village Hall, on the left. The Chidham Women's Institute meet monthly in the hall – also held here are antique markets and other passing events.

Chidmere House at Chidham is a Tudor house probably built by a wealthy yeoman. The house took its name from the village pond alongside which originated as a marl-pit dating back to Norman times or further. There is little recorded history of the building until the 17th century. It was at one time two cottages and later as a farmhouse was owned by the Edes family who built the beautiful 17th century Westgate House in Chichester, which until recently was the West Sussex Records Office.

When Mr H. L. Baxendale bought the house in 1930, half of it was a ruin. He restored the house in the following six years as well as creating the gardens into the beautiful area it is today. His son, Tom Baxendale, shown in the lower photograph, now owns the property and regularly opens the garden to the public under the National Gardens Scheme.

Cobnor House, Chidham, a Regency house which stands at the southern end of the Cobnor peninsula, overlooking Chichester Harbour. It was owned by the late Martin Beale, a local farmer, magistrate and benefactor in the area and his family still retain the estate. The old painting was done by Miss Walker, daughter of the Rev. G.A. Walker, who was Vicar of Chidham, between 1858 and 1870. The house was purchased by Martin Beale's father in 1919. The modern photo shows Martin Beale with his wife Ann, taken shortly before his death in 1990.

In the early 1900s the house lay empty for many years. During that time there are tales told of the house being haunted and lights being seen at night from the windows.

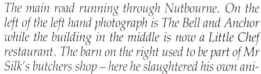

The main road running through Nutbourne. On the left of the left hand photograph is The Bell and Anchor while the building in the middle is now a Little Chef restaurant. The barn on the right used to be part of Mr Silk's butchers shop – here he slaughtered his own ani- *mals and made his meat deliveries covering a large area from Emsworth to Bosham. His shop and the barn were pulled down in the 1950s in order that the road could be widened; at the time this road was part of the main coastal highway between Portsmouth and Brighton.*

The right hand top photo is further along the same road – little changed in the last 80 years except for the road surface; tarmac instead of gravel. Ruth Wakeford's mother (see Introduction) lived in the house in the middle of this photograph. On the left is another section of the same road with the Nutbourne Stores on the right, which together with the building next door, have remained relatively unchanged. Inevitably there are many more buildings around and almost all the trees have gone, while the motor vehicle has replaced the horse-drawn one.

The school at Thorney Island, taken at the beginning of the century. The building was demolished in 1938 as it was in the path of the runway when Thorney Island was taken over by the RAF as an air station.

Now the island is almost a village in itself with married quarters, shops, leisure facilities and a medical centre. After the RAF left, the Vietnamese boat people were billeted here for a short time. Now the army uses the base and the new school is mainly for the children of the service personnel stationed here.

50 ACRES £2,750
OLD SUSSEX MANOR HOUSE.
Lounge hall, 2 other good reception rooms, 7 bedrooms
(accommodation easily enlarged), ample domestic offices,
stabling and outbuildings.

APULDRUM.

Rymans at Apuldram was built in 1410 by William Ryman, a prominent merchant and lawyer, with stone brought from Ventnor in the Isle of Wight. Rymans is only a few yards from the sea; indeed the same stone was also used to build the Bell Tower of Chichester Cathedral. The old photograph is from the cover of a brochure when the house was for sale in 1919. The print is of Rymans in the 18th century.

The old village school on the main road at Birdham. Since the new school was built in 1964, the old school, built in 1817 and enlarged in 1874 for 220 children, has been converted into five houses, as can be seen in the modern photograph.

The Hard at the end of The Street at Itchenor. The old photograph, taken in 1910, shows boats pulled up on the hard for scrubbing. The thatched cottage in the middle of the old photograph was 'Ferryside', occupied by George Haines. George, when he settled in Itchenor, in addition to his ferry duties, ran a thriving yacht maintenance business and employed some thirteen men to help him. He knew the name and outline of just about every boat in the harbour – he lived on well into his eighties.

His old home is now the Harbour Master's Office. The cottages on the left built by the Duke of Richmond in the 18th century look much the same, even to the chimney pots, while the house on the far right, Jetty House, now occupied by Mrs Flavia Nunes, looks little changed.

Richmond cottages in The Street at Itchenor, built for a few hundred pounds for his estate employees in the 18th century by the Duke of Richmond & Gordon, who built Itchenor Park. Today the same cottages sell for thousands of pounds. Outwardly from The Street they look the same, but behind many additions have been made, which of necessity include bathrooms; the old privies at the bottom of the garden are now used as tool sheds, that is if they have not rotted away.

The Street at Itchenor with the 18th-century cottages on the left. The road leads now to the shore with a hard at the end from which boats are launched.

At No. 5, The Street, lived Mrs Haines, the widow of John Haines. She ran the Rose Tea Rooms from her home in Gordon Cottages, which are the second block of houses on the left. (The other block is Richmond Cottages, for both were built by the Duke of Richmond & Gordon.) The Haines family became absorbed in the life of Itchenor when George Haines married Rebecca Rogers whose family had lived here for many generations.

The name Itchenor came from the Saxon Icca tribe and was at one time known as Icenore. 'Street' is an indication that the Romans were around this area and is a derivative from the Roman word 'Strata' – a road.

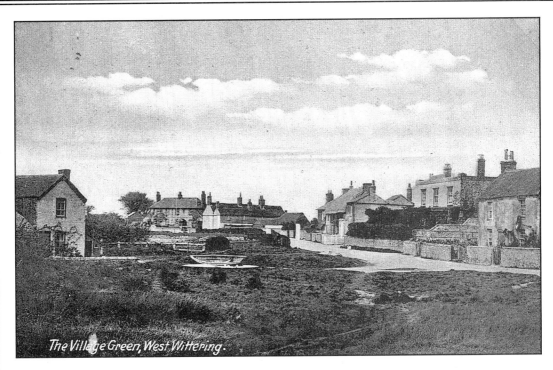

The Village Green, West Wittering.

The village green at West Wittering. In the old photograph, a postcard dated 6th August, 1929, the sender of the card ('Eva,' she signed herself) 'went in for a dip this morning' for 'the camp is not far from the sea.' Eva goes on to say 'It is very pleasant down here but very quiet.' Addressed to Mrs Davies in Southsea, she suggests to Dearest Gert that she might visit them in West Wittering – 'you could possibly get a cheap ticket to Chichester.' Today West Wittering might be quiet in the winter, but in August The Green is thronged with visitors.

Pound Road in West Wittering, formerly The Street, with the church in the distance. The old postcard, which may have been taken after 1911, for it has a George V stamp on the back, shows the church in the background. The wall on the immediate left is that of the old pub The Dog and Duck which is now a private house. It was for a short period a tea room. Further down the road is the school, little altered since it was built in 1837, except for some additions.

DAILY TOILS

OF NECESSITY, the motivation for working is to provide man with food and the other essentials of life. When man first came to the area of Chichester Harbour, when Britain was attached to mainland Europe, he would have found everything for his daily needs; wild animals as well as fruits and plants in plenty. But this area would have been difficult to farm once the wandering tribesmen wished to settle down to cultivate the soil. When man discovered how to make iron, he was then able to till the heavy soil and cut down the forests. The first knowledge we have of serious trading in Chichester Harbour is from the Romans although undoubtedly trading must have gone on long before the first century.

When the Roman harbour at Fishbourne was found as a result of aerial photography, also found were rocks and stones from eastern Mediterranean countries brought as ballast in ships which brought spices. These rocks were unloaded from the vessels in Fishbourne and the ships returned to their own countries laden with the corn grown in this area. (Some of these 'ballast' rocks are also to be found in the Trippet wall at Bosham.) This corn was famous throughout the Roman Empire for its excellent quality; corn that fed the Roman armies of north-west Europe. By the middle of the 18th century, the amount of corn exported from Chichester Harbour was equal to that shipped from all the other ports of Sussex and Kent.

The Roman galleys also brought marble with which to make the mosaics for the wealthy Roman citizens who chose to settle in this part of the world. With an agreeable climate, plenty of cheap labour, good soil to produce the high quality corn, good grazing for the sheep, from which came wool for clothing, and iron available a few miles away in the Weald, the Roman gentry would have found everything they needed for a comfortable and peaceful life with their families; this would account for the number of Roman villas which have been, and continue to be, found all along the coastal area.

Middle Ages

Henry I, who was the son of the Conqueror and ruled England from 1100–1135 A.D., granted a charter to the citizens of Chichester to sell their goods through the ports of Wittering and Horemouth – an old name for the harbour, though also the name of the Harbour mouth. Throughout the Middle Ages wool and hides were exported although the first official reference to the export of goods from the harbour was in 1226. By the 15th century, wool was the principle export.

By a Charter of 1681, Dell Quay was to be the only port in the harbour permitted to land or discharge any goods for the city of Chichester.

Shipbuilding

Although undoubtedly boats from dug-out canoes to King Harold's fleet of longboats, as well as ships for the Armada, had been built in Chichester Harbour for centuries, it was not until the end of the 18th century, with the launching of the 'Chichester' (the first of her name) that Chichester Harbour was to see the start of shipbuilding on a large scale. The fifth-rater of 44-guns the 'Chichester' was launched from Itchenor on March 10th, 1785. Three other navals ships were launched from Itchenor in the late 18th and early 19th centuries. In addition the 'Transit' was launched from there in 1800. She was the first ship to be built with the clipper characteristics and her sail plan was so advanced that it foreshadowed fore and after rigging. She was offered to the Navy but Their Lordships of the Admiralty refused to entertain a ship of such revolutionary design. She proved a splendid cargo carrying vessel with her additional speed and was the forerunner of the famous clipper ships.

There were two shipyards at Bosham building schooners of up to 500 tons, the last of these being the 'Good Hope' which was launched in 1903 from the Apps Shipyard by Quay Meadow.

Also launched from Mariners Shipyard at Bosham in 1922 was the 'Prince of Wales', the largest flat-bottomed passenger river vessel in the world at that time, built for the Southend Navigation Co. for their passenger service on the River Thames.

Ships were built at Birdham in the early 18th century – perhaps they took part in some of Nelson's naval battles!

Boat building continues, until quite recently in Bosham but now only at Itchenor where the

Northshore Boatyard turns out 25-50ft sailing yachts. Employing over one hundred people, Northshore have sold vessels to all parts of the world including India and Japan. Other shipyards in the harbour have turned to maintaining and repairing pleasure yachts, of which there are some 8,000 either on swing moorings or in one of the many marinas.

Fishing

Fishing was another occupation that must have gone on in the harbour ever since men first came here in boats. Bede in his Ecclesiastical History of the English Nation tells of how St Wilfrid came to Selsey in 681 A.D. and taught the locals how to fish. No doubt they knew something about this occupation before then but he probably taught them how to improve their skills. We learn that the Lords of the Manors around Chichester Harbour found difficulty in getting anybody to answer the call to arms after the month of August when the mackerel season started and the fish had to be salted to provide food for the winter.

In Bosham have been found Mediæval walls made of oyster shells – another industry which must have existed for centuries, for at the begin-

ning of the 20th century Bosham was second only to Whitstable in the oyster trade. The trade had been purely local until 1846 when the London, Brighton and South Coast Railway came through Bosham and it was then possible to get the oysters to London in one day. At the end of the 19th century there were some 40 oyster boats – Bosham punts – operating out of Bosham but this trade ceased in about 1920 when slipper limpets began to attack the molluscs. Today the industry is slowly reviving but most of the oysters go to France where they fetch a higher price than in England!

Watercress Growing

The clear spring water from the South Downs has for centuries provided the main ingredient for watercress growing in the Nutbourne and Chidham areas. This too had only a local market until the arrival of the train service when it was possible to get the cress to London and other places in one day.

Brick-making

Brick-making was another industry which has ceased during the last century. The heavy clay

was excellent for making bricks and the Romans had at least one brick-making works in the harbour. Roman tiles have been found in the Dell Quay area. With the departure of the Romans, the art of brick-making in this country was lost until Flemish brickmakers were brought to this country in the 15th century. There was a brickworks that operated until the beginning of the First World War on Bosham Hoe. There are some people who are convinced that this particular brickworks was originally a Roman one – it would certainly appear to have been in operation before 1625 as bricks of the type made prior to that year have been found in the area. It was not possible to reach this brickworks from Bosham and the brickmakers were rowed across to Furzefield from Itchenor. There was also a brickworks at Chidham until the 1930s.

The Mills

Milling was another industry within the harbour. There were mills at Bosham, Nutbourne, Fish-bourne (two), Dell Quay, Chidham (believed to be Neolithic) and Birdham. The latter, a tidal one was built in 1768 and was the last to operate in the harbour, closing in the 1930s. The Birdham mill pond was turned into a boat anchorage and was the forerunner of the modern marinas.

Salt Pans

Salt-making was another industry that undoubtedly went on for many centuries. The remains of salt pans have been found in Dell Quay, Appledram, Birdham, Chidham and Bosham.

Today

Today there is little commercial business that is not associated with the recreational activities of Chichester Harbour; there is the one exception – fishing. A few fishing boats come into the harbour for oyster dredging, but that is all. With the advent of the train, the motor vehicle and the better roads, shipping goods by sea around the harbours is no longer an economic trade.

Quay Cottage at Bosham, once two 18th-century fishermen's cottages, is now one house. About once every 40 or 50 years, the tide rises high enough to cover the floorboards of the downstairs rooms. Even at normal high tides the seawater reaches half-way up the wall, as shown by the marks on the wall in the old photograph.

This house is next door to the mill and in the foreground of the old photo is the water that has passed through the millwheel.

Not surprisingly, bearing in mind its position, it is thought that the building was used for smuggling in years gone by!

This is the site of the Apps shipyard, one of a number of shipbuilders in Bosham. It was situated at the northern end of Quay Meadow. Here until 1903, were built vessels of up to 500 tons, which traded across the continent and around the coasts of Britain. The last large vessel to be built at the Apps yard was the 'Good Hope', which was launched in July 1903 and subsequently sunk by enemy action in 1916 during the first Great War.

Note the basket in the middle of the old photo, which was used as a form of scaffolding for, when placed under the stern of the vessel (which can be seen on the far right of the picture), it enabled the shipwrights to continue working on the vessel at all stages of the tide.

In the lower photograph the house called The Slip, which was built in 1913, can be seen. All this area was purchased by the 2nd Lord Iveagh (of Guinness fame) who became the Lord of the Manor of Bosham in 1919. His descendants still indirectly own the area in the form of a company, in which the family are shareholders; the Lord of the Manor is now a company.

The cottages along the waterfront at Bosham. The tide comes up twice daily, frequently covering the steps visible in the old photograph.

These houses, occupied for decades by fishermen, had their scullery/kitchens on this, the sea side, with a hole in the floor through which everything went (no privy down the garden for these householders!) which was hopefully carried away to sea at high tide. Nowadays these cottages are owned by weekenders or retired people who, after paying very high prices for them, have modernised them, turning the former sculleries into delightful sea-facing living rooms; far removed from the 2/6d (12 pence today) a week rental paid by the fishermen of 1900!

The mill on the Quay at Bosham, which was one of the eleven mills owned by the Manor of Bosham according to the Domesday Book. Domesday was a register of all land and property compiled by order of William the Conqueror in 1086. Rebuilt in the 1960s in the same style and shape as before and using as much as possible of the old material, the mill is now leased to the Bosham Sailing Club who use the building as their Clubhouse.

The Mill House at Bosham, which at the time of the old photograph, was occupied by the miller. He also had milking cows which he grazed on Quay Meadow (on the left) or in the fields behind his house. He had a dairy in what is now the kitchen on the right of the building with the brook immediately outside. When the house was renovated a few years ago, under the floor of the old kitchen/dairy was found evidence of Roman occupation. The Victorian addition, seen in the old photo on the left of the house, was demolished at the same time. Also found along the boundary wall was the remains of a mediæval wall made of oyster shells.

It was just where the photographer stood for both photos that the locals obtained their water from the Brook. On the right of the two pictures is the west wall of the churchyard.

The Quay of Bosham with a ketch unloading alongside the dock and the milkman on the left making a delivery to the Mill from his cart. The raptackle looks outwardly similar although today the Quay is filled with dinghies and cars belonging to those yachtsmen who are lucky enough to have secured a mooring in Bosham Reach which they can reach after a few minutes' row from the Quay.

The Quay of Bosham which is owned by the successors of the 2nd Lord Iveagh (of Guinness fame) namely the Burhill Estate, who are now the Lord of the Manor. The Manor of Bosham owns all the land under the sea water up Bosham Channel as well as large tracts of land in Bosham village.

The Apps shipyard at Bosham, sketched by H. Boardman Wright (1888-1915) and printed from the original plate by Susanne Lowry in 1985. It shows the yard shed, to the left of which is where the schooners were built. This is a sketch and not a photograph. It would not appear to be very accurate as photographs taken at the same time show more buildings as well as a slipway. The house on the left in the modern photograph is The Slip, built in 1913, with the forge on the right used by the shipbuilders, a building of considerable age and left out of the sketch.

The mill pond at Bosham. In the old photograph there is the church tower in the middle with the back of the shipyard shed (see page 48) on the right. In the new photograph, Mill House can be seen on the left, which is hidden by trees in the old photograph. The church tower can just be seen through the trees in the new photograph. The pond is now filled with weeds and could pass unnoticed unless one knew where it was. The area to the right in both photographs is now the dinghy park for the Bosham Sailing Club.

LONG'S
Ales and Stouts.

Approved and Recommended by the
British Analytical Control . . . . .

Local Agent—HENRY FOLLETT,
Grocer and Provision Merchant,
HIGH STREET, BOSHAM.

The High Street in Bosham. The old photograph was taken in 1907 when it was Follett's Stores – there are still Folletts living in Bosham. The old buildings were demolished in 1947 and rebuilt as a grocery/wine shop – Hines' Grocery Shop. It has since been divided into two, one half being a tea room/clothing shop, the nearer half an art gallery. Above is a large self-contained flat, which, in 1947, was occupied by the owner of the grocery shop, Mr Hines. The little cottage to the right has acquired an additional window above the front door, as well as a porch.

A Hard across the top of Bosham Creek which led from the Mariners Boatyard, where the 'Prince of Wales' was built, to Gosportside. Mr Fowler, the builder, lived on Gosportside and the story goes that he became annoyed, when the tide was low, at having to walk all around the top of the creek and back (by the old school) at lunchtime, so he built this hard over the mud.

The old Bosham Bakery, a house now called Loafers, in Bosham Lane. The building was thought to be a pub before it was a bakery although it was probably only an ale house. There is a story, without any serious foundation, that this building was a toll house when monks occupied Critchfield House opposite and pilgrims, coming to the ancient church, had to pay an 'entrance fee' to the monks before being allowed to proceed further.

In the 1880s the Purvers ran the bakery and delivered bread daily around the village, from a hand-pushed cart – as seen in the old photograph. After the death of Mr Purver, his daughter and son-in-law, the Layzells, helped widow Purver to carry on the business. Unfortunately Mr Layzell was no expert in bread making, the business failed (caused it was said because Mr Layzell added mashed potato to the bread to make it whiter and was in trouble with the food authorities) and was sold to a brewery in Chichester – this may have been Sparkes whose name appears on the wall in the old photograph. For a while the building was used as a tea room.

Today Sheila (who is seen in the modern photo) and David Barton own the house. Sheila spends many hours looking into the history of the old building (which according to Mrs Eva Purser, grand-daughter of the Layzells had the ghost of a little old lady in grey) and David Barton was treasurer of the Parochial Church Council.

Laurel House, formerly the blacksmith's cottage, which has over its front door WMM 1697. Another cottage in the village, Tremyletts, built in a similar style, has WRM 1697 – these initials could be those of the builder or the owner of the cottages.

When this was the blacksmith's cottage, it was occupied by at least three generations of the Redman family over a period of more than 100 years. The Redman family also had a forge at Fishbourne (now a private house) where the horses of Lord Gifford were shod. A kinsman of the Berkeley family, and Lord of the Manor of Bosham, Lord Gifford lived at Old Park. It is probably members of the Redman family standing outside the cottage. The forge here can be seen to the left of the old cottage in the old photograph; this has now been demolished and is part of the drive to a house recently built to the rear of Laurel Cottage. Sally and Nigel Norcross-Webb, with their small son, who in the lower photograph stand outside the front door of the cottage, have done extensive restoration to the old building as well as building the flint wall to match the cottage.

Rectory Farm, Bosham (at one time known as Burnt-house), which the Strange family have owned for many generations.

In the old photograph Dorothy Strange, then aged 19, stands by the front door of the old 17th-century building. In the recent photograph Richard Strange, Dorothy's nephew, with his wife, Marian, and children, Alistair and Jenny, stand in front of a new porch. The door on the left has been bricked up.

Until recently Richard's father, Douglas, his wife Kathleen and brother Alan, lived here but Douglas has recently retired and the two families switched houses.

The fields of Bosham Hoe before 1913 being ploughed by Farmer Strange, his son and Tom Combes. Behind the men can be seen Combes Shipyard – now a flourishing business specialising in restoring old vessels. In the last war, the yard built lifeboats for ships. Before that barges brought sand and gravel here for Bosham.

Today the area is the highly desirable residential area of Bosham Hoe and Smugglers Lane where expensive houses have replaced the meadows of grazing cows and fields of corn.

The main road, which, within living memory was called the Turnpike Road, has changed much at this crossroads. This is a south view from The Swan Inn, with the Pound on the right. Any stray animals that were found wandering in the village were taken to the Pound, where the owners could claim them on payment of a fine. Afterwards the Pound became a garage, which was then demolished to make way for the roundabout in the modern photograph as this was the main road from Portsmouth to Chichester.

In 1988 this road was by-passed by a new one built about a mile north from here; this road is now a local one to serve the villages that run along the northern side of Chichester Harbour.

Shops in Station Road, Bosham. In the background is the station at Broadbridge, an area which was developed as a result of the Brighton and South Coast Railway going through Bosham in 1846. Here is Bosham Station Post Office, a newsagent and a grocery store.

The area between the shops and station, which has remained almost unchanged, was the coalyard but with the closure of the latter, a number of houses were built on the site, the road for which is called Arnold Way after a gentleman of that name who lived in the area.

The level crossing at the top of Drift Lane, Chidham. The Brighton and South Coast Railway which was built in 1846 and ran from Brighton to Portsmouth had no station at Chidham; the nearest station was Bosham. The house in the background remains unchanged but the level crossing keeper now has a nice little house, in front of which stands Mrs Jacqui Clark and her son, Ashley, daughter and grandson of the keeper, Mrs Carol Doe.

The Mill Pond at Nutbourne, which has now been drained and is used for grazing animals. There had been a mill here at least since 1086 when waters from the Ham brook (a name now given to the area north of Nutbourne) were used, although in 1327 it was noted that the mill sometimes stood still for want of water. In the middle ages, this area was a busy port, with a quay and the mill where trading vessels were to be seen regularly loading and unloading. Now the Nutbourne Marshes are a bird sanctuary with a few stone walls left standing to remind us of its former glory.

The blacksmith's cottage at Nut-bourne, where once the waters from the mill pond lapped at the door. The Jordan family were the last of many generations of black-smiths to work in the building. Here is George Jordan with his son – one of the photographs taken by John Metcalfe in the early 1900s. Today there is only a small stream and the cottage has been extensively renovated.

Now Englefield Antiques, the shop used to be the Fishbourne Bakery, run by the Blake family. Mr Blake ran a daily delivery service of fresh bread throughout Fishbourne and Bosham. Today the building is an antique shop which sells everything from antique furniture to galvanised bath tubs, such as were used in modest homes for the weekly bath in the kitchen for each member of the family on Saturday nights.

Above: A painting of the Mill at Dell Quay by R. H. Nibbs; the Mill is now converted into a private house.
Below: A sketch of the Mills at Fishbourne c.1850 by the same artist.

Dell Quay, which was for many years before the building of the Chichester Canal, the port for Chichester. Here goods for the city were transferred from boat to cart for delivery to the city. In the eighth century, Dell Quay was the seventh most important town in Sussex, after Bosham which was the sixth. While today the Quay is owned by the Chichester Harbour Conservancy for the storage of moorings, etc., the Dell Quay Sailing Club have built a new Clubhouse on the left from which, only possible at high tide, they conduct dinghy races.

Birdham Mill from the landward side. Here can be seen the lock gates into the tidal mill pond. This mill pond was turned into a marina after the mill ceased working and was the forerunner of the modern marina. Fuel and water are available for boats from the other side of the lock gates. The Birdham Pool is separated from Chichester Marina, which is home to some 1,000 boats, by a few houses and by the Chichester Canal.

Birdham Mill was the last of the tide mills. It was operating until 1935 when the buildings were sold to a yacht club. The Birdham Yacht Club was at one time situated in the building on the left in the old photograph, but this was burnt down some years ago. The Club then moved to the building immediately to the left of the 'Birdham Shipyard Ltd' notice in the modern photograph, but the lease of that building is now up and the owners of the building wish to sell. So the Birdham Yacht Club is at the moment without a clubhouse.

A barge sailing past Itchenor in the 1930s, probably on her way to Birdham or Dell Quay. Across the water is Bosham Hoe and Lower Hone on the Bosham peninsula.

In the modern picture, Toppers race in the same water. These photographs typify the change in Chichester Harbour – from commerce to pleasure boating.

In the old photograph George Haines, ferryman by adoption, proudly shows off his Anzani outboard. George was born in Portsmouth and spent many years at sea before settling in Itchenor and marrying Rebecca Rogers, whose family had operated the ferry across to Bosham for some 400 years – 4d (1½p.) at high tide and 3d (1p. +) at low tide. As the years went by, fewer people wished to go back and forth to Bosham. In 1964 George applied to the House of Lords to be allowed to discontinue the ferry – it had been a 24-hour a day job.

In 1976 the Chichester Harbour Conservancy started a ferry service again which operates during summer months only. There is a regular service between Bosham (Lower Hone) and Itchenor – yachtsmen can also be ferried to and from their boats.

Today Giles Cockburn is one of the ferrymen with an Evinrude outboard on the back of a dorey – the charge 50 times what it was in 1939!

Formerly North House in Chapel Lane, West Wittering, where the Willshire family lived for many years with the forge next door. Frederick Willshire was the last blacksmith and died in this house in June, 1968, at the age of 94. His daughters sold the house and built a bungalow next door which can be seen on the left in the new photograph. North House was one half of the building and has remained divided since – it is possible to identify some of the windows and doors in the two photographs – the old photo was taken in about 1900.

Mr and Mrs David Hoggard live in the right half of the building, Chapel Elms, and here Genny Hoggard poses in the garden with Olive Willshire, daughter of the last blacksmith. Tony and Mary Davies now live in the other half of North House which has an addition added to it on the far side.

The blacksmith's forge in Chapel Lane, West Wittering. Here two generations of the Willshire family carried on the trade of blacksmiths and in the old photograph John and Frederick Willshire are to be seen. The forge on the left was recently purchased by Kenneth and Sheila Townsend-Green and converted into a cottage. They have built a garage (outside of which is Kenneth Townsend-Green) this side of the vestry of the Methodist Church, seen in both photographs down the lane on the left.

Trickey Stores at West Wittering prior to 1931. The shop sold everything imaginable for those times. Mr Trickey was also a carrier. A carrier went daily to Chichester from West Wittering leaving at 9a.m. The journey took two hours. The carrier left Chichester again at 2p.m.

There were a number of subsequent owners of these stores, but recently the building was pulled down and now there is a group of new houses built on the site.

Coming into West Wittering along the main road from the north, one came to 'Potters', a shop that always appeared to sell everything, though there are shops opposite that sold other things. 'Potters' always had beautiful dahlias, when in season, grown a mile or so up the road.

Recently the whole complex shown in the old photograph was knocked down and a new building erected with a shop and cottages (bottom pic).

The uniform may change, but the charm remains the same.

ECCLESIASTICAL HISTORY

OF ALL the churches around Chichester Harbour, Bosham is the oldest; in fact it is the oldest building in which Christianity has been continuously preached in Sussex, although there are older church buildings than Bosham church in Sussex.

It is thought that the bases of the Chancel arch of the church may be all that remains of a Roman basilica that stood on the site. There is a story that Pudens, a Roman Governor of the area, who married Claudia, thought to be a daughter of Cogidubnus and also a Christian, had a villa in Bosham – and it is from Claudia and Pudens that St Paul sent greetings in his second Epistle to Timothy, Chapter 4.

The Ven. Bede in his Ecclesiastical History of the English Nation, tells of how St Wilfrid came to Sussex in 681 and found a Celtic monk named Dicul together with five disciples trying to convert the locals to Christianity without much success. The site of Dicul's monastery is thought to be the crypt of Bosham Church but there are a number of other spots in Bosham where Dicul might have had his cell.

The Parish Church of Bosham, the oldest of the churches around Chichester Harbour. Recent research has revealed that parts of the church, including two storeys of the tower, date back to the late ninth century. The first stage of the chancel, together with a further two storeys of the tower, was added in about 1050 A.D. at the time of Earl Godwin, father of King Harold. In the walls of the old tower could be seen Roman bricks, but in 1988 the tower was re-rendered in limestone and the Roman bricks are no longer visible.

The spire was added in the 15th century. From the west-facing Saxon window at the top of the tower, it is possible to see the harbour entrance at East Head, West Wittering – should the villagers have maintained a lookout from this window, it would have been possible to have warning of any possible raiders and for the villagers to repair to the church with their families and animals and bolt the church door. There is a legend that on one such occasion, the pirates did not stop at just looting the village, but broke down the church door and stole one of the church bells. Rowing away with the bell in their boat, the bell fell through the bottom of the boat at a place now named Bell Pool. Now whenever the church bells ring, the stolen bell answers from the deep!

Bosham

The first part of Holy Trinity, Bosham, was built in about 850 A.D., and was enlarged during the reign of King Canute (995-1035). In the following one hundred years, the church was again enlarged twice, culminating in the addition of the lovely east window in 1120 A.D., said to be the finest example of an Early English window in this country.

The Manor of Bosham was owned by Godwin, Earl of Wessex (990-1053) and father-in-law of Edward the Confessor. On Godwin's death it passed to his son, Harold. Harold had been crowned King of England at Westminster Abbey and so when Harold was killed at the Battle of Hastings, William the Conqueror inherited all Harold's property. Bosham thus became a royal manor.

Included in the Manor of Bosham were Chidham, Appledram, Thorney and Funtington. Thorney and Appledram are both Norman 12th-century churches, while Chidham, Itchenor and West Wittering churches are all Early English. None have changed much since they were built all those years ago.

St Cuthman

St Mary's, Chidham, is associated with St Cuthman, famous for the story that he arrived in Steyning from the west pushing his elderly mother in a wheelbarrow. The 'west' may have been Chidham for there is a Chapel of St Cuthman in the church and there was mentioned in 1635 a St Cuthman's field – identified today as Cullimer's field on Cobnor Farm.

The very simple little 13th-century church of St Mary's, Chidham. Little has been changed externally, even when some restoration was done in 1864. Chidham was part of the Manor of Bosham and as such part of the estate of the Bishop of Exeter until the Reformation. Bosham was a royal manor and after the Conquest, William gave the ecclesiastical part of Bosham, which included Chidham, to Edward the Confessor's chaplain, Osbern, who became Bishop of Exeter.

Thorney Island

The Parish Church of St Nicholas, Thorney, was built originally in 1100 by Bishop Warlewaste. In the Chancel only a small section remains of the original church. There was possibly an even earlier building as reference is made to the church at Tornei (Thorney) in the Domesday Book of 1086, a register of all lands and property in England ordered by William the Conqueror. The church as it stands today is mainly 13th century.

Thorney church is a large church which gives one an idea of what a large farming community there must have been there. Thorney was an island, only accessible by foot at extremely low tide, until 1870 when a causeway was built across to Hermitage, near Emsworth. Being part of the Manor of Bosham, Thorney was included in the gift given to Osbern, Bishop of Exeter and previously Chaplain to Edward the Confessor. Bosham, together with Chidham and Thorney were thus under the jurisdiction of the Bishop of Exeter until the dissolution of the monasteries in 1548.

Appledram

The church of St Mary's, Appledram (or Apuldram) was part of the Manor of Bosham until the 12th century when Henry I, son of William the Conqueror who had founded an abbey on the site of the famous battle, gave Appledram Manor, which included the church, to the monks of Battle Abbey. The corn grown on their land at Appledram was taken by sea to Hastings and thence by cart to Battle Abbey, for it would have been a near impossible task to transport the grain by land, such was the state of the roads – or the lack of them – in Sussex!

William de Warlewaste, Bishop of Exeter, had founded a college in Bosham with six canons, one of whom was given the prebend of Appledram, which gave the incumbent about £20 a year. Wiliam of Wykeham, founder of Winchester College and New College, Oxford, was a holder of the prebend of Appledram in 1363. Until 1417 the dead of Appledram had to be buried in Bosham. As a result of a petition brought by the Appledram parishioners, who found the road 'tedious and dangerous from floods and inundations' this practice was stopped, though whether as in the case of Funtington, the incumbent in Bosham had to be paid a penny for each adult and half-a-penny for each child buried in Appledram instead, is not recorded. The patronage of Appledram is now with the Dean and Chapter of Chichester Cathedral.

St Mary's, Appledram.

The Parish Church of St Nicholas at Thorney Island painted in 1892. This church, built by Bishop Warlewaste, is largely of the 13th century, although there are two sections of wall which are 12th century. Thorney was an island until 1870, when a causeway was made joining it to the mainland. Thorney was part of the lands owned by Earl Godwin, Earl of Wessex and father of King Harold (of 1066). Godwin incurred the displeasure of his son-in-law, Edward the Confessor, and fled the country from Thorney. But the dispute would appear to have been short-lived for Godwin returned to England the following year. Thorney Island was part of the Manor of Bosham which was given to Bishop Osbern of Exeter by William I, the Conqueror.

The area was, until 1976, an R.A.F. station. In the churchyard are buried soldiers and airmen of many nationalities who were killed in this area during the 1939-45 war. St Nicholas ceased to be a Parish Church in 1981 and became a Chapel of Ease. The church is now used by the army, who occupy the old air station, although non-service personnel still attend the church services.

St Peter's Chapel

St Peter's Chapel at New Fishbourne is the newest of all the churches in the area; it was built between 1244 and 1253 in fields belonging to the Manor. There is little left of the old building today except for a 13th-century lancet window in the chancel. It would seem possible that pilgrims from the continent on their way to visit the shrine of St Richard at Chichester Cathedral rested here, for they left several small crosses scratched on the north-east corner of the building. The majority of the present building was constructed in 1821 while the last addition was in 1973 when the north transept was added. The church was lit by oil lamps until 1950.

Now the church of St Peter and St Mary, it is some distance from Old Fishbourne, for although the village of Fishbourne had been established some 200 years before the original chapel was built, there would appear to have been no room for such a building nearer to the inhabitants. New Fishbourne is part of Chichester while Old Fishbourne was, until 1984, within the parish of Bosham.

Obviously the parishioners of Old Fishbourne found it quite a distance to walk to their Parish Church in Bosham for in 1906, the Vicar of Bosham arranged a short service on the second Sunday of each month to be held in Fishbourne Village School. This would have been the old school next door to The Black Boy Inn (now called Mallards Hotel).

Fishbourne has now been formed into its own parish, with its own Parish Council, amalgamating the two areas of new and old Fishbourne. Within sight of Chichester Harbour, the parishioners can walk from their homes across a field to the church, although a large car park has been made west of the church.

The Hundred of Manhood

A prince of Wessex, Caedwalla, granted in 683 A.D. to St Wilfrid, the Bishop of Northumbria, a parcel of land where he could establish a monastery. This area of land formed the Hundred of Manhood and included the villages of Birdham, Earnley, West and East Itchenor, Selsey, Sidlesham and East and West Wittering.

The most recently built of these churches is Birdham, which was built in the 14th century and is one of the smaller churches in the area. It was given by Queen Elizabeth I to the Dean and Chapter of Chichester Cathedral with whom it has remained – like other churches in the Manhood. The Lord of the Manor is the Bishop of Chichester.

St James, Birdham.

St Peter & St Mary, Fishbourne.

Itchenor Church Interior.

St Nicholas, West Itchenor.

The Church of St Nicholas, West Itchenor (East Itchenor, which was between West Itchenor and Birdham, was destroyed by fire to prevent the spread of the plague) is named after the patron saint of seafarers. The church stands on a mound; at one time the sea came almost up to the church but many years ago a dyke was built some 200 metres north-east of the church and the land inside the dyke reclaimed. There are stories that before the dyke was built when vessels could go right up to the church, smugglers made use of the church cellars for storing their contraband.

West Wittering has within its parish Cakeham Manor, which was at one time the popular residence for the Bishops of Chichester. The Bishop remains the Lord of the Manor. It is interesting to note that the boundaries of lands given to St Wilfrid by Caedwalla have changed very little over the centuries and although the Bishop was at the time of St Wilfrid in Selsey and transferred to Chichester at the time of William I, the Church Commissioners retain the Lordships of the area.

There are Roman Catholic churches at Bosham and Nutbourne – the Church of the Assumption of Our Lady at Bosham is a very new building, while the R.C. church at Nutbourne is a converted barn.

There is a small 19th-century Methodist Chapel on the main road through Nutbourne, while on the outskirts of West Wittering there is a Methodist Chapel in Chapel Lane built in 1811.

At Bosham, non-conformists met in one of the oyster barns until the Congregational Church was built in Bosham Lane in 1837. With the amalgamation of two denominations, it is now the United Reformed Church.

St Peter & St Paul, West Wittering.

The Church of St Peter & St Paul,
West Wittering.

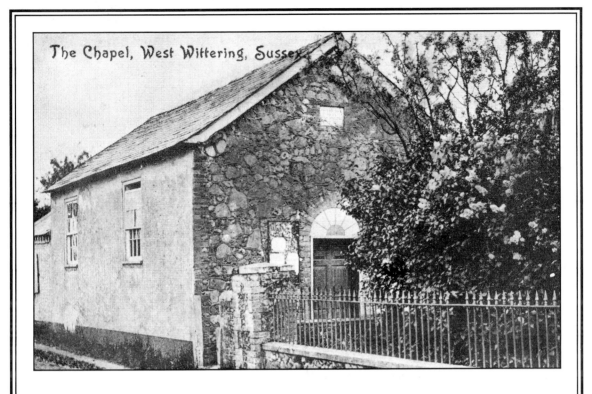

The Chapel, West Wittering, Sussex

The West Wittering Methodist Church in Chapel Lane has changed very little in the last 90 years. Built in 1811, enlarged in 1858, it started as 'Bethesda' (a Bible Christian denomination) then became in 1907 the United Methodist Church and finally in 1932 the Methodist Church.

The Willshire family have always been closely associated with this little church – the blacksmith's forge where three generations of Willshires operated is next door and the family continues to live next door – but not in the blacksmith's cottage. In the recent photograph, Mrs Ethel Lambeth (née Willshire) bicycles home past the church.

The interior of Bosham Church in 1862.

Nutbourne's Methodist Church in the background amongst the trees – the trees and little cottages are the same today.

The interior of Holy Trinity, Bosham, in the early 1900s. Note the old heating boiler on the left and the oil lamps.

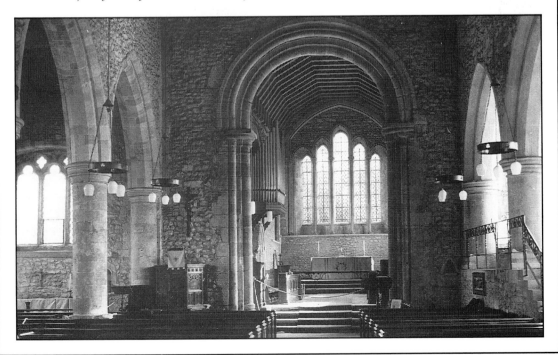

LEISURE TIMES

IT IS difficult to imagine now a time without radio or television but it was only in the 1930s that wireless became commonplace and the 1950s when a television set would be found in every home. Before that entertainment was self-made and grandfather, during the long winter evenings by candlelight, entertained the family with the stories that had been told to him by his father and grandfather.

The real centre of village life was the 'local' (pub), though this was mainly a male domain. Here teams from the various 'locals' competed against each other playing such games as dominoes, cribbage, shove halfpenny and table skittles. There were also singing groups, particularly in the Bosham pubs.

Bosham had the Bosham Blackbirds who met in the upstairs room of The Anchor for their regular singing sessions. Bosham and West Wittering had their 'tipteerers' or Christmas mummers who acted Mummers' plays at Christmas time. There were also the Morris dancers who went around the villages, usually performing outside the pubs – for obvious reasons! Dancing and watching dancing are thirsty occupations.

Then most villagers had their cricket and football teams, which competed against each other. Bosham even had a ladies' cricket team at the beginning of this century.

There were also the fairs and fêtes. The Sloe Fair in Chichester in October drew villagers from all around the neighbourhood who, climbing into the farmers' and carriers' carts in their best clothes and hats, went off for a few hours of fun. The fairs also visited the villages on specific days of the year; on Regatta Day in Bosham, the fair

was set up on Quay Meadow as well as Bull's Field opposite The Anchor.

Bosham had the Sunday School treat in May when the fair came to a particular field, now remembered in Fairfield Road and Fairfield House. Fairfield Road is where the Roman Catholic Church has been built.

In West Wittering there was a time when a fair was held in the garden of The Dog and Duck, a former local pub, now a private house.

Regattas were another annual excitement – before the modern concept of sailing clubs were formed, the regattas consisted of fishing boats from the various villages around Chichester Harbour competing against each other. The events appear to have taken place usually at Bosham, though in some years they were held at Itchenor,

when the different fishing fleets competed against each other. 1907 was one such year.

Fêtes were also one of the big events of the year; in West Wittering they held one either in the field alongside the school or on the village green. Bosham had a mammoth affair that went on for four or five days. Train excursions from Portsmouth and Brighton were advertised, the band of the Royal Sussex Regiment attended and such notable figures as the Bishop of Chichester and the Duke of Richmond & Gordon were reported to have attended. Until after the 1939-1945 war, everyone worked five-and-a-half days a week so with the exception of the Bank Holidays, of which there were about six a year, there were only Saturday afternoons and Sundays on which to indulge in any of these activities.

412 CHIDHAM LANE

The Barleycorn taken some years ago by Mr H. L. Baxendale of Chidmere. Except for the cars outside it has changed little, but at the time that the old photograph was taken, the customers were mostly locals who came on foot – today the customers are largely passing traffic who come by car and stop for a sandwich and a glass of beer.

Actor Peter Trubshawe, famous for his wonderful handlebar moustache, was once the landlord of this pub, as was Alan Arnedale, a well-known Liverpool footballer.

The High Street of Bosham, showing The Anchor Bleu and, two doors away, The Ship. The Ship is now a private house but The Anchor is still a popular inn, which it has been for some hundreds of years. It was not always the smart place it is today; popular with all the tourists who pour into Bosham to visit the church and enjoy the seascape which can be viewed from the balcony on the far side of the building. During the last war, The Ship was an officers' club where the artist, Whistler, painted a mural, which is now sadly disintegrating. This must be the last of Whistler's paintings for he was killed a few days later in the invasion of France in June, 1944.

Street End, Bosham. In the distance can be seen the creek, pictured at low tide. Normally the water covers the creek twice a day at high tide, but during the high spring tides twice a year the water covers the road here. (Note the high steps into the gardens to prevent the sea-water getting into the gardens and houses.)

On the left in the old photograph can just be seen the end of the words 'Gloucester Inn': this building, the whitewashed building in the modern photograph, is now a private house called Gloucester House. Note the difference in the road surfaces – someone who was a child when this photograph was taken described the gravel road as a dust bowl in the summer and a mud bath in the winter.

The Quay at Bosham, which in the old photograph shows boats being loaded up for a sailing trip, the other shows a yacht being lifted out of the water at the end of the sailing season. Seamen from Bosham, who fished for oysters and mackerel during the winter months, during the summer formed the crews of amongst others, such famous yachts as 'Britannia', 'Westward' and the various 'Shamrocks'.

THERE WILL BE A REGATTA AT

Happy Bosham

ON THURSDAY SEPTEMBER 2ND

WRITE FOR PARTICULARS TO THE HON SECS
YE OLD ANCHOR INN, BOSHAM.

The Berkeley Arms, Bosham, an 18th-century building named after the Berkeley family who were Lords of the Manor of Bosham for some 400 years. In 1911 a bowls club was formed and met in The Berkeley.

More recently the British Legion met in an upstairs room of The Berkeley (until there were too many and the meetings were transferred to the village hall). The President of the British Legion at one time was Peter Trubshawe, the actor. Another 'regular' was Eileen Robey who lived next door to the pub in Rose Cottage and was a sister of the comedian, George Robey.

There have been many changes to the building, including the loss of its thatch.

Itchenor Sailing Club Regatta. The old photograph was taken of the Regatta held on 27th August, 1932, and shows youngsters getting their boats ready for racing. The same situation pertains in the modern photograph of the Junior Regatta in August, 1989. Except for the type of dinghies, little has changed even to the excitement of the children and the exasperation of the parents! Across the water northwards is Lower Hone, Bosham.

The old photograph is of the starting platform at the Itchenor Regatta in August 1934. On the far left of the picture is Mrs Lowles whose husband became Commodore of the Club in 1937 and afterwards Admiral. Jimmy Gilbert is next to her; he was one of the founders of the Club and also Hon. Sec. from 1927-1933. Third from the right was Dr Menzies and two away from him was Mr Lear who was Vice-Commodore of the Club from its beginnings in 1927 until 1934.

During the war, the building was occupied by the Army who built an anti-aircraft gun platform a few yards from the pre-war starting platform. After the war, this became the starting platform for races and it was from this point that the 1989 Junior Regatta races were started and finished.

Bob Massey, a former Commodore of the Club, is on the far right with Murray Fox on the far left.

In the old photograph Sunbeams (with the Vs on their sails) and XODs race off the Hard at Itchenor. While these fixed keel yachts, together with Swallows, still operate from the Itchenor Sailing Club, due to the congestion in this part of the harbour, the races are started from committee boats anchored further down the harbour in less crowded conditions.

The first XODs, wooden-hulled fixed keel boats, were built in 1907. They still remain popular in the Solent; there are some 40 boats in the Itchenor Fleet alone; other fleets are at Cowes in the Isle of Wight, Lymington, Yarmouth and Poole.

Old House at Home, West Wittering.

The Old House at Home at West Wittering. This was an ale house until! The Dog and Duck ceased to be a pub and The Old House took over that role. The building has been considerably enlarged over the years as can be seen from the chimney pots – the two far ones are the original ones as seen on the old photograph and the windows have been thrown out in the front. Judging from the dress of the ladies, the photograph must have been taken before 1914. The road surface has also changed.

The church fêtes of Bosham. The old photograph is of the Dutch Fête of 1906 held in the Vicarage garden in Walton Lane. The fête raised £217 to repair the church. The vicarage has now been converted into flats and is called Walton House. The gardens of the vicarage are now part of Oakcroft Nurseries.

The fêtes lasted many days and drew crowds from miles around. In the old photo Roley Heaver (2nd from left) and Maude Heaver (2nd from right) pose with others in front of one of the stands. The Heaver family still live and work around Bosham.

The new photo was taken at the 1989 church fête, which has been held for many years in the Manor House Gardens by the kind permission of Mrs Leviah Harden. It shows the white elephant Hoe Stall which was started after the last war by the late Lady Allen who owned the Bosham Hoe Estate. Mrs Margaret Godber continues to organise this stall which, in Lady Allen's time, was manned by residents of The Hoe. Here the Godber's neighbour, David Bowker, is busy persuading onlookers to make a purchase. Among them are Mrs Gill Beaumont (in check shirt) and Mrs Pam Tomlins (in pleated skirt).